UNSTOPPABLE JOHN

How John Lewis Got His Library Card—
and Helped Change History

WRITTEN BY PAT ZIETLOW MILLER
ILLUSTRATED BY JERRY JORDAN

VIKING

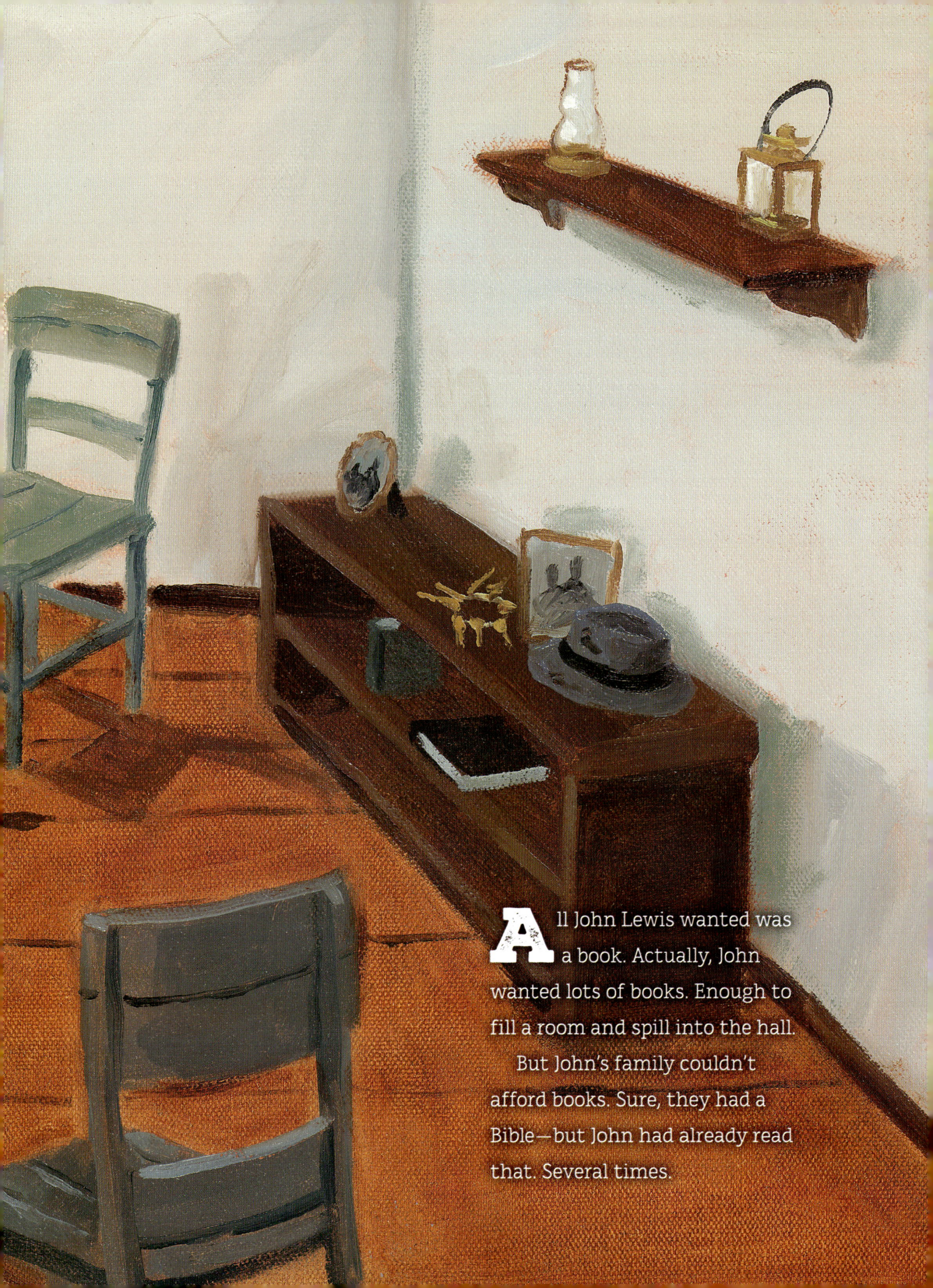

All John Lewis wanted was a book. Actually, John wanted lots of books. Enough to fill a room and spill into the hall. But John's family couldn't afford books. Sure, they had a Bible—but John had already read that. Several times.

John's grade school didn't have many books, either. Just a few tired hand-me-downs. And he'd already read those, too.

You might think you can solve John's problem. You might think John should go to the library. Libraries have books. And borrowing them doesn't cost a thing.

John knew that. He knew the library had more books than he could ever read.

But John knew something else, too. Most libraries were for white people.

And he was Black.

These days, of course, libraries are open to everyone. But there were different laws when John was young.

Those laws weren't fair. But that didn't stop John. John believed everyone should be able to borrow books.

And he knew someone had to do something to help things change.

Maybe that person could be him.

So, John walked to the library. He opened the door,
stepped inside, and asked for his own library card.

John knew the librarian would tell him "No." And she did.
But that didn't stop John. John sent a letter to the library
asking them to lend books to everyone.

He waited and waited. But the library never wrote back.

So, John read whatever he could find. Newspapers. Advertisements. Signs.

They had words, but they weren't books.

When John went to college, he looked for books.

And found them! A whole roomful. John almost lived in that room.

That solved at least one of John's problems.

But because of unfair laws, John still couldn't get a public library card to read all the books he wanted.

There were lots of things John couldn't do because of those racist laws.

Like . . . eat at a restaurant.

Watch movies at a theater.

Sit in the front of a bus.

Or register to vote.

John knew Black people should have the same opportunities as white people, and that laws should never be based on race. So, John read more. And learned more. John shared what he learned with other people who knew the laws weren't fair. He listened to what they knew, too.

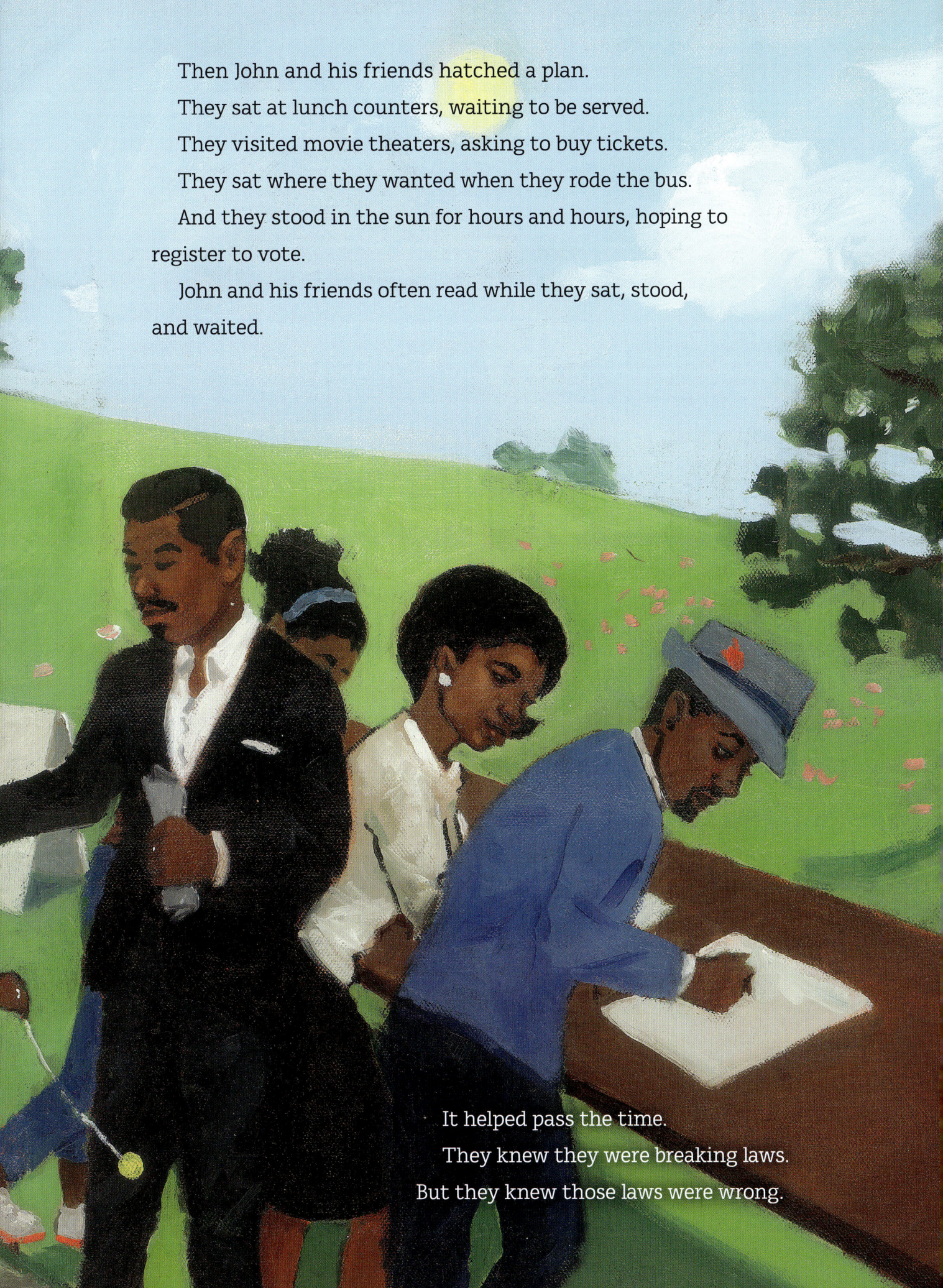

Then John and his friends hatched a plan.

They sat at lunch counters, waiting to be served.

They visited movie theaters, asking to buy tickets.

They sat where they wanted when they rode the bus.

And they stood in the sun for hours and hours, hoping to register to vote.

John and his friends often read while they sat, stood, and waited.

It helped pass the time.
They knew they were breaking laws.
But they knew those laws were wrong.

Again and again, they were told "No." Again and again, they came back and asked for what they knew was right. They did not stop. No matter how long it took.

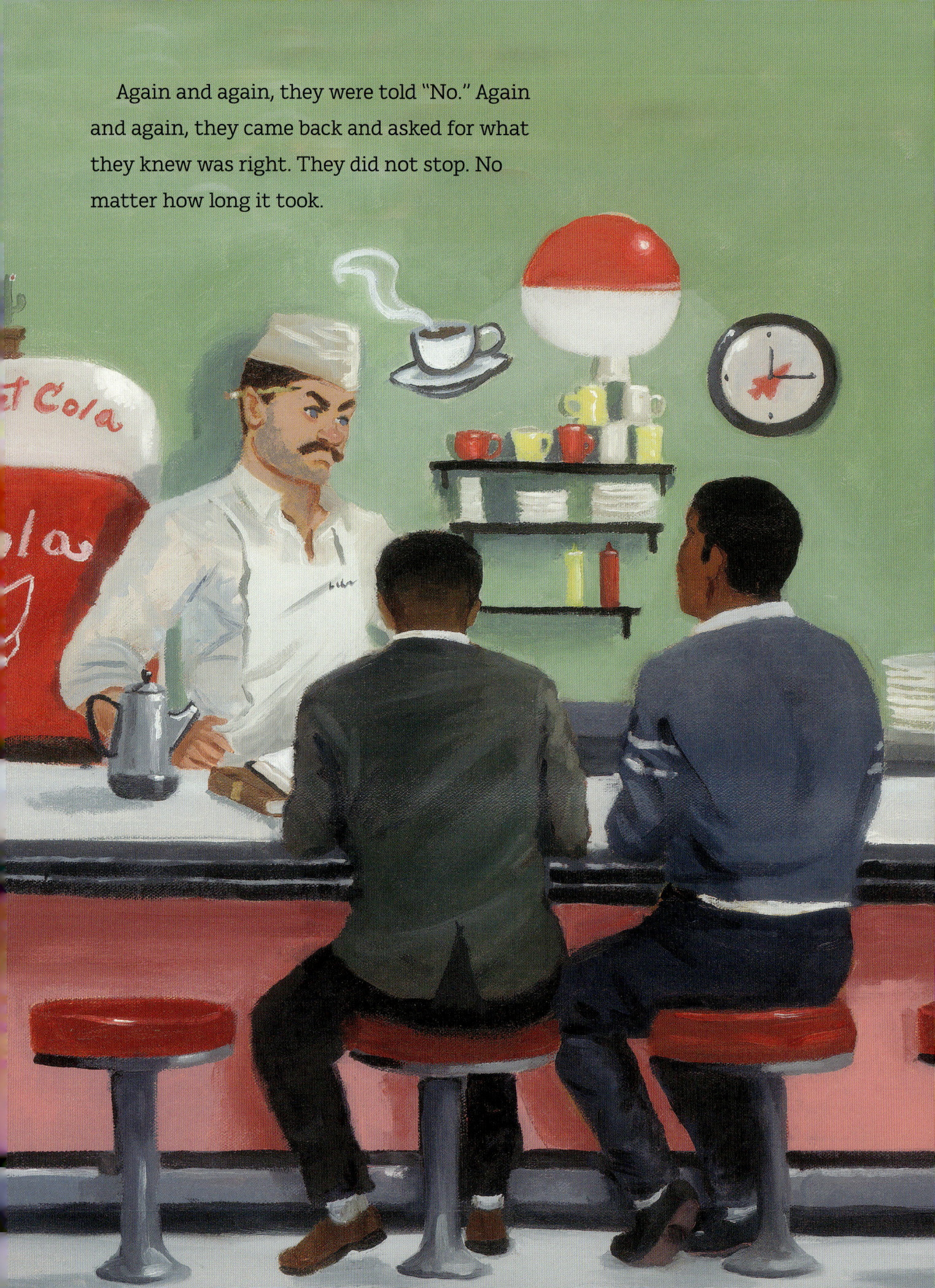

Many people wanted John and his friends to back down. They liked the laws the way they were. Sometimes those people sent John and his friends away using words that seemed nice but really weren't.

"I'm sorry. I can't sell you a ticket."

"This lunch counter is closed."

Other times, people didn't even pretend to be nice. They yelled terrible things. Or hit, kicked, and spit on John and his friends.

Even that didn't stop John. No matter what other people said or did, John didn't argue or fight back—even when someone hurt him enough to send him to the hospital.

He didn't give up. And he didn't back down.

Sometimes people became so angry and violent, the police got involved. But the police didn't arrest the people being mean. Oh no. They arrested John and his friends.

It wasn't fair, but that didn't stop John. He kept asking for equal rights even though he was arrested many times.

Sometimes John and his friends marched. Big groups of people, all together.

In Nashville, Tennessee. Washington, DC. Selma, Alabama.

They hoped people would realize how unfair the laws were.
And work to change them.

Of course, John got tired. But that didn't matter.
John still did not stop.
Slowly, slowly, the laws changed.

Black people could eat at restaurants.

See movies.

Sit anywhere on the bus.

Vote in elections.

Even get library cards.

John was thrilled. But he kept right on working. There was more to read. More to do. More to learn. John did take one break, though.

He married a librarian who loved books as much as he did.

And then unstoppable John kept keeping on. He joined the city council in Atlanta, Georgia.

He ran for the US House of Representatives in Washington, DC. And won.

Wherever he was, John worked for equal rights. He even wrote a book about it.

Then John returned to his hometown library. The one that told him "No" when he was sixteen.

He gave a speech. Hundreds of people came. When John finished, the librarians gave him a library card. Forty-two years after he'd first asked for one.

John wrote another book. And another.
And another. And another.

One of those books won an award. When John
accepted the award, he told a story. About how
a boy who couldn't check out books grew
to one day write them.

As John talked, he
almost cried.

Not long after, John received a note in the mail.
It was from a Virginia library he'd never visited.

A library card fell out. So did a message from the
librarians there. They congratulated John
on his work. And invited him to stop
by and see them. Anytime.

Because stopping by is *not*
the same as stopping.

John Lewis never stopped working to make our country better. He supported laws to keep people safe. Laws to help them when they were sick. Laws to protect their right to vote.

And John never stopped reading. He knew there was always more to learn. That's why he made sure his home had enough books to fill a room and spill into the hall.

Just like he'd always wanted.

AUTHOR'S NOTE

When sixteen-year-old John Lewis walked into the whites-only Pike County Public Library and asked for a library card in 1956, it was the start of a remarkable journey.

John was inspired by Rev. Martin Luther King Jr., whom he'd heard speak about nonviolent civil protests. John didn't get his card that day, but his request—and the letter he wrote afterward stating that the library should be for everyone—was his first protest.

Others followed. While he was still in college, John became a leader in the Civil Rights Movement, joining the Student Nonviolent Coordinating Committee (SNCC). He trained others in nonviolent protest techniques and organized efforts that led to the integration of lunch counters and movie theaters in Nashville, Tennessee.

John took a national role when he became a Freedom Rider, working to integrate bus stations at great personal risk. He was beaten and arrested multiple times. But the Freedom Riders' work ended bus station segregation.

As SNCC chair, John was part of the Big Six who planned the March on Washington. Other members were James Farmer of the Congress of Racial Equality, Martin Luther King Jr. of the Southern Christian Leadership Conference, A. Philip Randolph of the Brotherhood of Sleeping Car Porters, Roy Wilkins of the National Association for the Advancement of Colored People, and Whitney Young Jr. of the National Urban League.

John spoke at the March on Washington, where an estimated 250,000 people advocated for civil rights legislation. At twenty-three years old, he was the day's youngest speaker.

John also led registration efforts for Black voters in a peaceful fifty-four-mile march from Selma, Alabama, to Montgomery, Alabama, which law-enforcement officers stopped with violence on the Edmund Pettus Bridge in what would later be called Bloody Sunday. Officers fractured John's skull, but he finished the march later that month under medical supervision.

Despite the pain and setbacks, John never considered turning back. In his memoir, *Walking with the Wind*, he writes: "When I first got involved in the movement as a teenager, I recognized that this struggle was going to be long, hard and tedious, and that I would have to pace myself and be patient where necessary, while continuing to push and push and push no matter what."

That pushing led to the Civil Rights Act in 1964 and the Voting Rights Act in 1965. Among other things, the Civil Rights Act meant John could use any library in the nation. John finally returned to the Pike County Public Library (which had been renamed the Troy Public Library) in 1998 when he—at long last—received the library card he'd asked for all those years ago.

JOHN LEWIS'S LIFE

1940—Born February 21 near Troy, Alabama.

1953—Attends Pike County Training School in Brundidge, Alabama.

1956—Asks for a library card at Pike County Public Library in Troy, Alabama, at age sixteen. His request is denied.

1957—Attends American Baptist Theological Seminary in Nashville, Tennessee.

1958—Studies nonviolent resistance with Rev. James Lawson.

1959—Joins the Nashville Student Movement.

1960—Helps organize peaceful sit-ins at Nashville department store lunch counters and stand-ins at Nashville movie theaters that lead to the counters and theaters eventually being open to all.

1961—Joins the Student Nonviolent Coordinating Committee (SNCC). Graduates from American Baptist Theological Seminary. Becomes a Freedom Rider and is beaten in Rock Hill, South Carolina, and Montgomery, Alabama, in an effort to integrate interstate bus terminals. Arrested for the first of at least forty-five times.

1962—Attends Fisk University to pursue religion and philosophy degrees.

1963—Elected chairman of SNCC and moves to Atlanta. Speaks at the August 28 March on Washington.

1964—Helps lead Freedom Summer voter registration in Mississippi. Civil Rights Act passed.

1965—Leads march for voting rights on March 7 in Selma, Alabama, with Rev. Hosea Williams. Is beaten and hospitalized with a fractured skull during Bloody Sunday. Participates in subsequent march from Selma to Montgomery under medical supervision. March leads to passage of the Voting Rights Act.

1966—Joins the Field Foundation and helps provide grants to child welfare and civil rights organizations.

1967—Graduates from Fisk University. Works as community organizer for Southern Regional Council.

1968—Marries librarian Lillian Miles.

1970—Becomes executive director of the Voter Education Project. Helps register nearly four million new Black voters.

1975—Receives Martin Luther King Jr. Peace Prize. Featured in *TIME* magazine story "Saints Among Us."

1976—Adopts son, John-Miles.

1977—Loses race for US House of Representatives. Joins ACTION, a federal volunteer-coordinating agency.

1981—Elected to Atlanta City Council.

1986—Elected by the Fifth Congressional District of Georgia to US House of Representatives.

1998—Publishes *Walking with the Wind: A Memoir of the Movement*. Holds book signing at Troy Public Library and receives the library card he was denied in 1956.

2001—Receives John F. Kennedy Profile in Courage Award for Lifetime Achievement.

2011—Receives Presidential Medal of Freedom.

2012—Publishes *Across That Bridge: Life Lessons and a Vision for Change*, an essay collection.

2013—Publishes *March: Book One* with Andrew Aydin and Nate Powell, a graphic novel of John's civil rights experiences.

2013—Arrested after protesting for immigration reform on the National Mall. This was at least his forty-fifth arrest.

2015—Publishes *March: Book Two* with Andrew Aydin and Nate Powell, a graphic novel of John's civil rights experiences.

2015—Commemorates the fiftieth anniversary of Bloody Sunday in Selma, Alabama, with then-president Barack Obama, former president George W. Bush, and thousands of others.

2016—Wins National Book Award for *March: Book Three* with Andrew Aydin and Nate Powell, a graphic novel of John's civil rights experiences. Receives a library card from the Fairfax County Library in Virginia with a note from the librarians congratulating him on the award and inviting him to visit anytime.

2017—Wins four awards from the American Library Association for *March: Book Three*—the Coretta Scott King award for best children's book by an African American author, the Michael L. Printz Award for excellence in young adult literature, the Robert F. Sibert Informational Book Award for most distinguished informational book for children, and the YALSA Award for Excellence in Nonfiction for Young Adults.

2019—Diagnosed with advanced pancreatic cancer.

2020—Dies July 17 in Atlanta, Georgia, at age eighty.

To John Lewis, with respect and gratitude —P. Z. M.

To all my family for their love and support. Especially my wife, Nyra. —J. J.

LEARN MORE

Asim, Jabari. *Preaching to the Chickens.* New York: Nancy Paulsen Books, 2016.

Aydin, Andrew; Lewis, John; and Powell, Nate. *March: Book One.* Marietta, Georgia: Top Shelf Productions, 2013.

Aydin, Andrew; Lewis, John; and Powell, Nate. *March: Book Two.* Marietta, Georgia: Top Shelf Productions, 2015.

Aydin, Andrew; Lewis, John; and Powell, Nate. *March: Book Three.* Marietta, Georgia: Top Shelf Productions, 2016.

Bausum, Ann. *Freedom Riders: John Lewis and Jim Zwerg on the Front Lines of the Civil Rights Movement.* Washington, DC: National Geographic, 2005.

Cline-Ransome, Lisa. *Fighting with Love: The Legacy of John Lewis.* New York: Paula Wiseman Books, 2024

Dowdey, Kathleen; Johnson, Chas. Floyd; Benson, Lillian E.; Schner, Charles A.; Kambon, Camara; and Lewis, John. "John Lewis-Get in the Way," PBS, 2017.

Eliopoulos, Christopher and Meltzer, Brad. *I Am John Lewis.* New York: Rocky Pond Books, 2023.

Haskins, Jim and Benson, Kathleen. *The Story of Civil Rights Hero John Lewis.* New York: Lee & Low Books, Inc., 2019.

Haskins, Jim and Benson, Kathleen. *John Lewis in the Lead: A Story of the Civil Rights Movement.* New York: Lee & Low Books, Inc., 2006.

Leslie, Tonya. *The Story of John Lewis: A Biography Book for Young Readers.* Emeryville, California: Rockridge Press, 2021.

Lewis, John. *Walking with the Wind.* New York: Simon & Schuster, 1998.

Lewis, John. *Across That Bridge: Life Lessons and a Vision for Change.* New York: Hyperion, 2012.

Meacham, Jon. *His Truth Is Marching On: John Lewis and the Power of Hope.* New York: Random House, 2020.

Pinkney, Andrea Davis. *Because of You, John Lewis: The True Story of a Remarkable Friendship.* New York: Scholastic Press. 2022.

Porter, Dawn. "John Lewis: Good Trouble," Participant Media, 2020.

Sapet, Kerrily. *Political Profiles John Lewis.* Greensboro, North Carolina: Morgan Reynolds, 2009.

School Library Journal. "A New Library Card for Rep. John Lewis | Picture of the Week," Dec. 8, 2016

VIKING
An imprint of Penguin Random House LLC
1745 Broadway, New York, New York 10019

First published in the United States of America by Viking, an imprint of Penguin Random House LLC, 2025

Text copyright © 2025 by Pat Zietlow Miller
Illustrations copyright © 2025 by Jerry Jordan

Visit us online at PenguinRandomHouse.com.

Library of Congress Cataloging-in-Publication Data is available.

ISBN 9780593524909

10 9 8 7 6 5 4 3 2 1

Manufactured in China
TOPL

Design by Lily K. Qian and Ellice Lee
Text set in KarloSerif

Art created with oil on canvas